PENNY DREADFUL

THE ONGOING SERIES

VOLUME 3 **THE VICTORY OF DEATH**

BASED ON THE SERIES CREATED BY

JOHN LOGAN

TITAN COMICS

MANAGING AND LAUNCH EDITOR
Andrew James

COLLECTION DESIGNER
Dan Bura

PRODUCTION ASSISTANT
Rhiannon Roy

PRODUCTION CONTROLLER
Peter James

SENIOR PRODUCTION CONTROLLER
Jackie Flook

ART DIRECTOR
Oz Browne

SALES & CIRCULATION MANAGER
Steve Tothill

PRESS OFFICER
Will O'Mullane

BRAND MANAGER
Chris Thompson

ADS & MARKETING ASSISTANT
Bella Hoy

DIRECT SALES & MARKETING MANAGER
Ricky Claydon

COMMERCIAL MANAGER
Michelle Fairlamb

HEAD OF RIGHTS
Jenny Boyce

PUBLISHING MANAGER
Darryl Tothill

PUBLISHING DIRECTOR
Chris Teather

OPERATIONS DIRECTOR
Leigh Baulch

EXECUTIVE DIRECTOR
Vivian Cheung

PUBLISHER
Nick Landau

Penny Dreadful – The Ongoing Series
Volume 3: The Victory of Death
Regular SC ISBN: 9781785861437

Published by Titan Comics. Titan Comics is a registered trademark, of Titan Publishing Group, Ltd., 144 Southwark Stre London SE1 0UP, UK. All rights reserved. ©2017 Showtime Networks Inc. All rights reserved. SHOWTIME is a regist trademark of Showtime Networks Inc., a CBS Company. All rights reserved.

No part of this publication may be reproduced, stored in a retrieval system, or transmitted, in any form or by a means, without the prior written permission of the publisher. Names, characters, places and incidents featured i publication are either the product of the author's imagination or used fictitiously. Any resemblance to actual pers living or dead (except for satirical purposes), is entirely coincidental.

A CIP catalogue record for this title is available from the British Library. First edition: February 2019

10 9 8 7 6 5 4 3 2 1

Printed in Spain.

PENNY DREADFUL

BASED ON THE SERIES CREATED BY
JOHN LOGAN

WRITTEN BY
CHRIS KING

ART BY
JESÚS HERVÁS

COLORED BY
JASON WORDIE

LETTERED BY
ROB STEEN

EDITOR
LIZZIE KAYE

PENNY DREADFUL

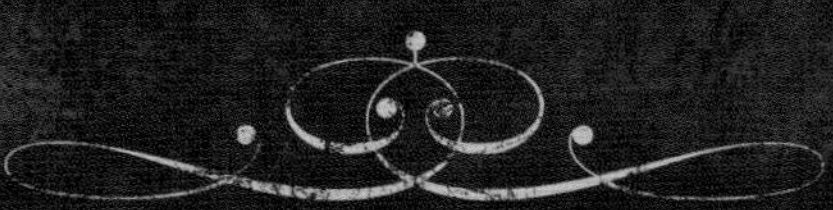

An ill wind blows through the streets of London...

Vanessa Ives' body has been inhabited by the ultimate evil, Satan, as the hordes of hell rampage through the streets of London. Ethan, still grieving for the love of his life, has committed an act that will surely lead to the ultimate destruction of mankind... unless they can find the eternal flame, the only thing that can put an end to the horror that has befallen humanity.

With so much at stake, and time of the essence, Catriona Hardtegan and Victor Frankenstein are charged with gathering their scattered troops, all the while battling demons and the Nephilim, in a desperate attempt to put on a show of force when they hunt down the immortal scourge of souls, and their last hope for redemption... the elusive Dracula.

YOU DECEITFUL BITCH! OU TRULY ARE THE MASTER OF LIES, USING VANESSA TO MANIPULATE ME!
NOW, NOW, MY DEAR. THIS SHOULD BE A JOYOUS OCCASION! OUR BABY GROWS NSIDE OF ME. YOU HAVE GIVEN E EXACTLY WHAT I CAME HERE FOR... A CHILD THAT WILL BE BORN OF FLESH AND BLOOD. IT WILL BE THE ANTICHRIST, RULER OF THIS WORLD... FOREVER.
I WILL SEND YOU BACK TO ***HELL*** BEFORE THAT HAPPENS!
YOU WOULDN'T KILL THE MOTHER OF YOUR CHILD, WOULD YOU, ETHAN? LET US RULE THIS WORLD TOGETHER, AS A FAMILY. JOIN US.
FUCK. YOU.
OU HAVE BLOOD YOUR HANDS. THE RY FIRST LIFE YOU SEALED A DEAL WITH WE ARE ETERNALLY WINED. THINK OF ME YOU DO YOUR MISS ES... WE BELONG ETHER. I'M THE ONLY E THAT WILL EVER LOVE YOU.
VANESSA WAS WHOLLY GOOD AND TRUE... YOU ARE PURE EVIL.
HERE'S EVIL OU AS WELL. OK INTO THE NESS OF YOUR T. ACCEPT ME TOGETHER WE LL RULE THIS WORLD.
NEVER!

THEN YOU GIVE ME NO CHOICE BUT TO END YOU, HERE AND NOW.
CHACK

YOU FOOL...
WHY DIDN'T YOU SAY "YES"? WE COULD HAVE BEEN A FAMILY. GOOD BYE FOREVER, MY LOVE.
MASTER SATAN, THE WOLVES ARE STILL ATTACKING.... WE ARE--
NONE OF THAT MATTERS NOW. THE WOLF OF GOD IS DEAD, BUT NOW I CARRY HIS CHILD, THE FUTURE RULER OF MANKIND. TAKE ME AWAY FROM THIS WRETCHED PLACE.
THERE IS STILL LIFE IN YOU... JUST HOLD ON, I WILL BRING YOU HELP.

BEFORE MR. RENFIELD DIED HE TOLD ME WHERE WE CAN FIND DRACULA.
THEN LET'S GRAB ETHAN AND LEAVE TH HOUSE OF HORRORS O AND FOR ALL!
CATRIONA, OVER HERE... ETHAN IS UP THESE STAIRS!
ETHAN IS JUST UP THOSE STAIRS.
HOW ARE YOU SO SURE?
THE DEAD TELL ME THINGS.
...SOMETIMES YOU SCARE ME.
HURRY, HE IS RUNNING OUT OF TIME!
ETHAN!

TIME TO DIE LIKE THE OLD DOG YOU ARE.
FWASH
RUSH
CHACK
BOMP

ASHES TO ASHES AND DUST TO DUST, YOU SON OF A BITCH!
CHA
THAT'S A BLESSED KNIFE, BURNING YOU WITH THE HOLY SPIRIT. THERE'S A SPECIAL PLACE IN HELL FOR MONSTERS LIKE YOU. MAY GOD HAVE MERCY ON YOUR SOUL, IF YOU EVEN HAVE ONE.
WHAM
KRRRR

YOU WILL O LONGER BE TROLLED BY THIS RSE, MR. GREY. IT'S OVER.
LORD GOD, I ASK THAT YOU GUIDE MR. GREY TO YOUR LIGHT. MAY HE FINALLY FIND PEACE AND HAPPINESS WITH YOU. AMEN.
WE WILL ALWAYS HAVE OUR WALTZ, DORIAN GREY. REST IN PEACE.

WELCOME, LORD OF DARKNESS, TO YOUR NEW HOME. UNFORTUNATELY, THERE WAS SOME DISCONTENT ABOUT YOUR ARRIVAL. BUT WE TOOK CARE OF THAT. PLEASE, FOLLOW ME.
YOU WILL BE PROTECTED HERE AS YOU AWAIT THE BIRTH OF OUR SAVIOR.
YOU HAVE DONE WELL, MY MOST DEVOTED SERVANT. MY CHILD, YOUR FUTURE KING, SHALL BE BORN BY THE NEXT FULL MOON.
SO SOON... BUT HOW?
THE BLOOD OF TEN THOUSAND WARRIORS RUNS THROUGH MY VEINS. THE CHILD FEEDS OFF OF MY LIFE-FORCE, DARKNESS FILLING ITS SOUL AS IT GROWS. NOW, HAVE YOU DONE AS I REQUESTED?
YES, LORD.
THOSE WHO STAND BEFORE YOU WILL CIRCLE THE GLOBE IN GREAT SHIPS, PROCLAIMING YOUR WORD. THE WORLD WILL SOON KNOW THAT YOUR CHILD WILL BE BORN TO RULE US ALL.

HOLY HELL!
I COME IN PEACE. I'M ON YOUR SIDE AND AM UNARMED. WE NEED YOUR HELP... IT'S ETHAN. HE HAS BEEN SEVERELY WOUNDED.
ETHAN... WHERE? TAKE US TO HIM!
MY SON! IS HE ALIVE?
YES, BUT HE'S LOST A SIGNIFICANT AMOUNT OF BLOOD. HE REQUIRES PROPER MEDICAL ATTENTION, BUT I FEAR MOVING HIM WILL CAUSE GREATER DAMAGE.
SO, WHAT DO WE DO?

I MUST GO TO MY OFFICE AND COLLECT AS MANY SUPPLIES AS POSSIBLE. CAT, I NEED YOU TO TAKE MY PLACE AND LOOK AFTER ETHAN. THE REST OF YOU, PLEASE PROTECT THEM AND MAKE SURE THEY REMAIN SAFE UNTIL I RETURN.
WHAT ABOUT YOUR SAFETY, DOCTOR? YOU SHOULDN'T GO OUT THERE ALONE.
I'LL BE FINE. JUST TAKE CARE OF MR. CHANDLER. I WON'T LET US LOSE ANOTHER MEMBER OF OUR FAMILY. I'LL BE BACK SHORTLY.
KAETENAY, YOU ARE INJURED AS WELL. LET ME EXAMINE YOU.
THERE'S NO TIME. IT'S NOTHING... DO NOT WORRY ABOUT ME, DOCTOR. I NEED YOU TO SAVE MY SON. GO!

IS THERE THING YOU NEED, MASTER?
IT'S ALL HAPPENING THE WAY I INTENDED. MY CHILD GROWS STRONGER AND STRONGER BY THE MOMENT. GOD'S POWER ON THIS EARTH IS WEAKENING.
IT'S TIME.

MASTER, WHAT ARE YOU DOING?

WITH THIS CHILD INSIDE OF ME, I HAVE UPSET THE BALANCE OF POWER. I HAVE TAKEN WHAT IS MINE FROM THE VINDICTIVE AND OBTUSE GOD. HE NO LONGER HAS POWER HERE.

KRRRRRRR
HEAR ME NOW, MY FALLEN BROTHERS AND SISTERS! JOIN YOUR MASTER LUCIFER ON THIS EARTH SO THAT WE MAY MAKE A NEW HOME. COME, MY DEMONS OF HELL, LET US BUILD OUR NEW WORLD!

ETHAN, WHERE ARE YOU? MOTHER JOAN? IS ANYONE HERE?
UGH.... OVER... HERE...
MOTHER JOAN, PRAISE THE LORD YOU ARE STILL ALIVE!
LILY, MY CHILD... YOU MUST LEAVE... SATAN MIGHT HAVE LOST THIS BATTLE, BUT HE IS WINNING THE WAR. A CHILD... SATAN... A *CHILD*.
CHILD? WHAT CHILD?
SATAN WILL GIVE BIRTH TO A CHILD. THE ANTICHRIST. MUST... STOP...
HOW IS THAT POSSIBLE?
IT'S ETHAN'S. YOU MUST... END THIS... BEFORE--
BEFORE *WHAT*? OH NO, PLEASE DON'T DIE, MOTHER, PLEASE! I AM SO SORRY THAT I BROUGHT THE DEVIL TO YOUR DOOR...

DOCTOR, GOOD TO SEE YOU ARE WELL. I WAS WORRIED SOMETHING MIGHT HAVE HAPPENED TO YOU. HURRY, COME INSIDE BEFORE YOU BREATHE ANY MORE OF THAT FILTHY AIR!
IT'S THE END OF DAYS OUT THERE.
IS THAT WHAT THE NEWSPAPERS ARE CALLING IT?
THEY BLAME IT ON THE WINDS, THE NASTY FOG AND ALL OUR FACTORIES CHURNING OUT SUCH TOXIC FUMES. BLOODY INDUSTRIES WILL KILL US ALL.
JUST STAY INSIDE UNTIL ALL THIS PASSES. I AM IN A HURRY, HAVE A PATIENT IN DIRE NEED OF MY ASSISTANCE. I AM JUST GOING TO MY OFFICE TO FETCH SOME SUPPLIES.
UNDERSTOOD, SIR.
IT IS GOOD TO SEE YOU, DOCTOR.

LORD HYDE, I'M SURPRISED TO SEE YOU HERE. IS EVERYTHING ALL RIGHT AT THE HOSPITAL? THE PATIENTS, THEY--
YES, I AM FULLY AWARE OF THE PATIENTS, DOCTOR. AFFECTED BY AN UNKNOWN AFFLICTION. BUT THE MOST HORRIFYING, YET GLORIFYING, EVENT TOOK PLACE. IT GAVE ME THE BREAKTHROUGH WE HAVE BEEN SEARCHING FOR... I DID IT, VICTOR!
DID WHAT?
THE FORMULA, I MASTERED THE FORMULA! WE TRIED SO MANY VARIATIONS - FROM ELECTRICAL CURRENTS TO HIGH DOSES OF MORPHINE. BUT IT WAS NEVER SUSTAINABLE. PATIENTS ALWAYS REVERTED BACK TO THEIR TYPICAL BEHAVIOR. BUT I SOLVED IT!
HOW?
I USED THE BLOOD OF A MONSTER...

HYDE'S FLASHBACK
"IT WAS YESTERDAY AFTERNOON, WHEN I WATCHED AS YOU AND THE OTHERS HASTILY EXITED BEDLAM, ABANDONING ME TO THE UNKNOWN HORRORS TO COME.
"I QUICKLY GRABBED MY FORMULAS AND HURRIED IN A POOR ATTEMPT TO CATCH YOU. BUT I WAS CONFRONTED BY THE MOST FASCINATING CREATURE.
"IT WAS THE MOST BEAUTIFUL, GROTESQUE REATURE I HAVE EVER SEEN. T REFUSED TO LET ME PASS.
YOU THERE... I SEE DARKNESS IN YOUR SOUL, BUT YOU ARE NOT A FOLLOWER OF OUR MASTER LUCIFER... WHY IS THAT?
"I STOOD THERE IN STUNNED SILENCE FOR A MOMENT AND THEN BUILT UP THE COURAGE TO FINALLY SAY...
I AM MY OWN MASTER. I AM JUST AS POWERFUL AS ANY DEVIL, OR ANY GOD FOR THAT MATTER.
LET ME SHOW YOU WHAT *TRUE* POWER IS...

THANK YOU FOR THE BLOOD, YOU BEAUTIFUL BEAST. YOU ARE EXACTLY THE SPECIMEN I HAVE BEEN SEARCHING FOR.
I WILL DESTROY YOU--
LEAVE HIM, HE'S NOT IMPORTANT. THE OTHERS ARE GETTING AWAY!
I WILL FIND YOU, DOCTOR, AND WILL RIP YOU IN HALF WHEN I DO.
NOT IF I FIND YOU FIRST.
"THAT BEAST AND HIS BRIDE LET ME BE. I TOOK THE SAMPLE OF BLOOD AND MIXED IT WITH MY OWN FORMULA. I WANTED TO CAPTURE THE POWER POSSESSED BY THAT MONSTER.
"SO, I USED IT ON MYSELF."
VICTOR, THIS IS THE BREAKTHROUGH WE HAVE BEEN WAITING FOR. I HAVE NEVER FELT SUCH STRENGTH AND DETERMINATION BEFORE. LET ME SHOW YOU WHAT REAL POWER FEELS LIKE.
I AM HAPPY FOR YOU, LORD HYDE, BUT I MUST LEAVE HERE IMMEDIATELY. I HAVE A SEVERELY INJURED FRIEND WHO NEEDS MY... WELL, PERHAPS OUR HELP. WILL YOU ACCOMPANY ME? WE CAN DISCUSS YOUR FORMULA ON THE WAY.

DEAR HEAVENLY FATHER, WE ASK THAT YOU RESTORE ETHAN TO HEALTH AGAIN. GRANT US THE GRACE TO ACKNOWLEDGE YOUR HOLY WILL AND KNOW THAT WHATSOEVER YOU DO, YOU DO FOR THE LOVE OF US. AMEN.
E BACK TO US, N. WE NEED YOU. I NEED YOU.
HE'S A FIGHTER, THAT'S FOR DAMN SURE.
THE ROLES WERE ONCE REVERSED. NOT VERY LONG AGO, HE STOOD BY MY SIDE AS DEATH BECAME ME. HE SHOWED SUCH MERCY. IT WAS A DARK PLAY I THOUGHT WE WOULD NEVER HAVE TO PERFORM AGAIN.
THERE'S A WONDERFUL HEBREW TERM THAT BEST DESCRIBES MR. CHANDLER... "HESED".
IT'S ONE OF THE MOST POWERFUL WORDS IN THE OLD TESTAMENT, THOUGH THERE IS NO SINGLE WORD IN THE ENGLISH LANGUAGE THAT BEST CAPTURES ITS MEANING.
SOME SCHOLARS BELIEVE IT MEANS "KINDNESS" OR "MERCY", BUT WHAT I BELIEVE BEST DESCRIBES "HESED" IS "LOYAL LOVE". THAT IS ETHAN'S DRIVING FORCE, LOYAL LOVE.
IN THESE DIRE TIMES, MAY WE ALL LEARN TO BE A BIT MORE "HESED", LIKE ETHAN.
WE WILL END ALL OF THIS SUFFERING, LILY. PLEASE BELIEVE ME.
CATRIONA, LILY... I BROUGHT HELP.

I BROUGHT ANOTHER BRILLIANT DOCTOR, LORD HYDE, TO HELP CARE FOR ETHAN.
HOW DARE YOU BRING THAT MAN HERE, FRANKENSTEIN? HE WAS ONE OF YOUR COHORTS WHO KIDNAPPED ME AND CHAINED ME IN YOUR DUNGEON!
MY DEEPEST APOLOGIES FOR MY HORRIBLE BEHAVIOR. THE MAN YOU DESCRIBE, WHO DID SUCH HEINOUS ACTS, IS GONE FOR GOOD. I PROMISE YOU... I HAVE NO ILL INTENTIONS.
YOU MUST TRUST ME, LILY. LORD HYDE IS BY FAR THE BEST DOCTOR I KNOW. HE WILL LOOK AFTER MR. CHANDLER.
WHAT ABOUT *YOU*?
I PROMISED ETHAN THAT I WOULD HELP PUT AN END TO ALL THIS EVIL. I WILL ACCOMPANY MISS HARTDEGEN TO TRACK DOWN DRACULA AND DESTROY THE DEVIL, ONCE AND FOR ALL.
SO BE IT. BUT I WILL NOT BE LEAVING ETHAN'S SIDE, NOT FOR A MOMENT.

MR. RENFIELD SAID THE NAME OF THE ISLAND IS ***MARBH BEO***...
"THE ISLE OF THE LIVING DEAD". I BELIEVE IT'S RIGHT ABOUT HERE, NEAR THE HIGHLANDS.
YOU KNOW OF THIS PLACE?
MOSTLY FROM GHOST STORIES AS A CHILD. DURING THE BLACK DEATH, HUNDREDS OF BODIES WERE DUMPED ON THE ISLAND, BUT MANY BELIEVE THEIR SPIRITS HAVE REMAINED.
FOR YEARS, PARENTS WOULD THREATEN TO SEND THEIR UNRULY CHILDREN, LIKE ME, TO THE ISLAND. MANY BELIEVE THAT WHEN EVIL MEN DIE, THEY WAKE UP ON MARBH BEO.
SO, HOW DO WE GET THERE?
WE BOARD A TRAIN FROM LONDON
EAD NORTH TO THE HIGHLANDS. THERE'S
N CALLED CHAILL NOT TOO FAR FROM THE
WHERE WE WILL HAVE TO SECURE A BOAT.
M NOT GOING TO LIE TO YOU, THIS IS GOING TO BE AN EXTREMELY DANGEROUS ENDEAVOR.
WE UNDERSTAND WHAT WE ARE -- ≡COUGH≡-- ≡COUGH≡.
KAETENAY, I FEAR YOU ARE UNWELL. YOU SHOULD STAY HERE WITH ETHAN AND HAVE THE DOCTOR LOOK AFTER YOU, TOO.
I AGREE WITH MY SISTER. YOU NEED TO REST. LET US GO WITH DOCTOR FRANKENSTEIN AND MISS HARTDEGEN.
YES, YES. THIS OLD PILE OF BONES ISN'T WHAT IT USED TO BE. I WILL PRAY FOR YOUR SAFE RETURN.

VICTOR, I AM UTTERLY SERIOUS WHEN I SAY THIS VENTURE COULD BE DEADLY. ARE YOU SURE YOU ARE UP FOR IT?
I HAVE LOOKED INTO THE DEEP ABYSS OF DEATH MANY TIMES BEFORE. I AM NOT AFRAID. BUT... THANK YOU FOR YOUR CONCERN. I'LL CHECK ON ETHAN, ONE MORE TIME, BEFORE WE GO.
SUCH BRAVADO BUT IT'S ALL FOR SHOW. I SENSE VICTOR'S FEAR. PROMISE ME YOU WILL LOOK AFTER HIM?
IT'S THE BRAVE AND THE FEARLESS ONES WHO WORRY ME. SOMETIMES A BIT OF FEAR IS EXACTLY WHAT YOU NEED TO SURVIVE. TRUST ME, I KNOW FIRST-HAND.
MALCOLM, I APPRECIATE YOUR FATHERLY CONCERN BUT WE HAVE A JOB TO DO AND I HAVE NO CHOICE BUT TO SUCCEED. MANKIND IS DEPENDING ON IT.
THEN I WISH YOU WELL, MISS HARTDEGEN. BRING BACK THE ETERNAL FLAME AND LET US DESTROY SATAN AND HIS DEMONS ONCE AND FOR ALL.
IN LATIN, THE FLAME IS CALLED *OMNIA LUMINARIA LUCIS*... THE LIGHT OF ALL LIGHTS.
MAY IT LIGHT YOUR WAY HOME SAFE AND SOUND, MY DEAR. GOOD LUCK AND GODSPEED.

HOW IS HE, DOCTOR?
HIS HEARTBEAT IS NORMAL. IT'S AS IF HE IS IN A DEEP SLEEP.
DREAM ON, MY LOVE, DREAM ON. AND WHEN YOU WAKE, MAY THIS NIGHTMARE WE ARE LIVING BE OVER.
LORD HYDE, IS EVERYTHING ALL RIGHT?
STEP BACK... I MUST BE ALONE. PLEASE, GIVE ME... A MOMENT!
MOMENT, THEN, ON'T YOU DARE LAY A N ETHAN WITHOUT ME T... I'LL BE LISTENING, GHT OUTSIDE THIS DOOR.

WE HAVE A BIT OF A JOURNEY AHEAD OF US...
IT WILL BE NICE TO TAKE A MOMENT TO BREATHE. LET'S TRY TO REST UP AS BEST WE CAN.
CAN'T IMAGINE GETTING MUCH SLEEP, BUT I WILL SURELY TRY.
TIME TO BOARD THE TRAIN, SISTERS.

COME, MY DEMONS OF HELL, AND JOIN OUR CONQUEST.
I NOW HOLD CLAIM TO THIS EARTH, FOR GOD HAS NO POWER HERE ANY MORE. WE SHALL SHAPE OUR NEW WORLD TOGETHER.
WE ARE HERE TO SERVE YOU, LORD SATAN.
ALL HAIL, SATAN.
SOON YOU WILL BE SERVING MY CHILD, THE FUTURE KING.
WHAT IS HAPPENING?

IT IS THE COMING OF THE BEAST. NOW, HAS MY FLEET DEPARTED?
YES, THEY HAVE. SOON...
...THE REST OF THE WORLD WILL BE UNDER YOUR CONTROL.

KNOCK KNOCK
LORD HYDE, CAN YOU HEAR ME? PLEASE, DOCTOR, LET ME IN. I NEED TO BE WITH ETHAN.
WHAT DO YOU WANT?
ARE YOU ALL RIGHT? YOU LOOK QUITE UNWELL. MAY I GET--
LEAVE ME BE, WOMAN. WHATEVER YOU DO, STAY AS FAR AWAY FROM ME AS POSSIBLE.
JUST NEED A BIT MORE...

UGH!
WHAT IS IT, LORD SATAN? IS EVERYTHING ALL RIGHT WITH YOUR CHILD?
I CAN FEEL HIM... THE WOLF OF GOD IS ALIVE. I CAN FEEL HIS SPIRIT COURSE THROUGH MY VEINS. I MUST HAVE HIM HERE BY MY SIDE.
ETHAN, I KNOV YOU CAN HEAR M WE ARE CONNEC THROUGH BLOC NOW...

Y SWEET, DO YOU REMEMBER WHEN E FIRST MET AT THE MARINER'S INN? AS LIVING ROUGH, A FALLEN WOMAN, WANTON AND MISGUIDED. YET YOU LOVED ME DESPITE MY CORRUPT NATURE. FOR YOU ARE WHOLLY GOOD, ETHAN CHANDLER.
PLEASE COME BACK TO ME.
INSIDE ETHAN'S MIND.
VANESSA... YOU'RE ALIVE.
WAKE FROM THIS CURSE. I KNOW YOU HAVE NEVER STOPPED LOVING ME. I AM YOUR DESTINY; OUR SOULS BELONG AS ONE.
YOU TOOK MY LIFE. YOU LET ME DIE IN YOUR ARMS IN ORDER TO SAVE ME FROM THE DARKNESS. ETHAN, I AM FREE. WE CAN FINALLY BE TOGETHER FOREVER.
SOON, WE WILL HAVE OUR FIRST-BORN. LET US FINALLY BE A FAMILY. I WAIT FOR YOU IN THE WHITE TOWER.

BACK TO REALITY.
VANESSA.
YES, I AM INSIDE YOUR THOUGHTS. COME TO THE WHITE TOWER, LET US BE ONE.
YOU'RE AWAKE! OH, THANK GOD. MY PRAYERS HAVE BEEN ANSWERED!
VANESSA. THE WHITE TOWER. THE WHITE TOWER.
WHERE ARE YOU GOING? YOU MUST REST. PLEASE, LIE BACK DOWN.
THE WHITE TOWER... VANESSA.
I'M SO SORRY BUT VANESSA... SHE'S DEAD.
HOW DARE YOU?! IT'S YOUR GOD WHO'S DEAD. VANESSA IS CARRYING MY UNBORN CHILD AND WAITS FOR ME AT THE WHITE TOWER.
ETHAN, STOP! COME BACK!

DOCTOR FRANKENSTEIN AND I HAVE FOUGHT DRACULA AND HIS FAMILIARS BEFORE. IT'S NO PICNIC.
WHAT IS THE NAME THAT YOU CALL THESE CREATURES?
VAMPIRES. HAVE YOU HEARD OF THE TERM HEMATOPHAGOUS? ANIMALS THAT ARE KNOWN TO CONSUME BLOOD. FOR VAMPIRES, SURVIVAL SOLELY DEPENDS ON THE BLOOD OF HUMANS.
THUS, WE MUST HEED CAUTION WHEN CONFRONTING DRACULA AND HIS VAMPIRE FAMILIARS. PURE DOMINATION IS WHAT THEY SEEK, AND THEY ARE TRULY MONSTROUS.
YOU DO UNDERSTAND WE ARE... WELL....
WHAT MY SISTER IS TRYING TO SAY IS WE ARE MONSTERS AS WELL. SOMETIMES IT TAKES A MONSTER TO DEFEAT ONE.

YES, BUT YOU BOTH ARE NEOPHYTES WHEN IT COMES TO THESE BEASTS. CAT AND I HAVE FACED THEM BEFORE. A MENTOR OF MINE ONCE TOLD ME VAMPIRES MOVE IN PACKS.
JUST WHEN YOU THINK YOU ARE CLOSE, THEY ARE GONE, TAKING OUR MOST BELOVED WITH THEM. FOR THE DEAD TRAVEL FAST.
SOMETHING ON YOUR MIND, SEDNA? YOU SEEM TO BE SOMEWHAT DISTANT.
MOVING IN PACKS... SOMETHING MY SISTER AND I KNOW WELL.
IT'S THIS ASH... IT HASN'T STOPPED FALLING. AS IF THE ENTIR WORLD IS ON FIRE.
IF I CAN PROVIDE ANY SOLACE, IT'S *NULLI DESPERANDUM, QUAMDIU SPIRAT* -- WHILE THERE IS LIFE, THERE IS HOPE. FAILURE IS NOT AN OPTION FOR DARKNESS AND EVIL HOLD NO DOMINION.
THAT IS WHY IT IS IMPERATIVE WE RECOVER THE ETERNAL FLAME AND SEND LUCIFER BACK TO HELL.
I HAVE TO SAY, ALL THIS TALK HAS MADE ME EXHAUSTED. ANYONE ELSE DESPERATE FOR A BATH AND SOME SLEEP?
YOU READ MY MIND. SHALL WE?
I BELIEV ONE MORE W IS IN ORDER. D WOULD YOU JOINING
I NEVER SAY NO TO A NIGHTCAP. SLEEP WELL.
GOOD NIGHT, GENTLEMEN.

VANESSA, I AM HOME.
YES, MY LOVE. NOW COME, JOIN ME AT MY SIDE AND LET US RULE THIS WORLD AS ONE.

ALL I WANT TO DO IS TEAR THESE CLOTHES OFF AND SUBMERGE IN A BOILING HOT BATH. I BELIEVE THE ONLY PLACE THIS SUIT I'M WEARING BELONGS IS ON A BONFIRE.
DO YOU HAVE ANYTHING ELSE TO WEAR?
WHEN FACING THE END OF THE WORLD, I TEND TO PACK LIGHT. ALL I HAVE IS THIS BLOODSTAINED TUXEDO.
ONE WOULD SAY I HAVE A MARTIAL SENSE OF STYLE, PRACTICAL AND FUNCTIONAL OVER PLEASING AND FANCY.
WELL, I CAME PREPARED. JOIN ME IN MY ROOM AND LET US FIND YOU SOMETHING PRACTICAL, YET PLEASING.
I'D WEAR A SACK AS LONG AS IT IS CLEAN.
I'M SURE YOU WOULD LOOK BEAUTIFUL IN ANYTHING.
PROMISE ME ONE THING... NO CORSETS. I DO ENJOY BREATHING FROM TIME TO TIME.

HOW DID YOU KNOW THAT SCARLET IS MY FAVORITE COLOR?
IT'S MINE AS WELL. I MADE IT MYSELF. WHEN IT'S -30°C IN MY VILLAGE, THERE IS NOT MUCH FOR US TO DO WITHOUT FREEZING.
SO NEEDLE PUSHING KEEPS YOU WARM?
THAT AND A FEW OTHER MORE VIGOROUS ACTIVITIES. NOW DON'T BE MODEST, GO AHEAD AND TRY IT ON?
NO ONE HAS EVER ACCUSED ME OF BEING MODEST.
YOU ARE ABSOLUTELY STUNNING.
NO ONE HAS EVER ACCUSED ME OF THAT BEFORE EITHER.
OUR HEART BEATING SO T. I CAN FEEL APING OUT OF OUR CHEST.
FORGET VAMPIRES, I AM MORE NERVOUS BEING ALONE WITH SUCH A BEAUTIFUL WOMAN.

SISTER, THE PLAN IS IN MOTION. TIME THIS TRAIN MAKES ITS FINAL STOP.
YES, SISTER. I WILL DO AS YOU SAY.
THEN GO NOW, FOR I HAVE SOME LITTLE BOYS TO PLAY WITH.
I MUST BE CLEAR ABOUT ONE THING, DOCTOR. SEDNA AND I ARE NOT FRIGHTENED OF THESE SO-CALLED VAMPIRES. TO ME THEY SOUND LIKE WALKING CORPSES WITH FANGS.
I'VE HAD ENOUGH WITH YOUR MASCULINE BRAVADO. THESE CREATURES' ONLY GOAL IS CONQUEST. YOU MUST--
GOOD EVENING, GENTLEMAN. SORRY TO INTERRUPT YOUR INTENSE CONVERSATION, BUT I COULDN'T HELP NOTICE THAT YOUR COMPANIONS HAVE LEFT YOU BOTH.
MY SISTERS LEFT ME AS WELL, SO MAY I JOIN YOU? I HATE BEING ALONE.
WE WERE JUST ABOUT DONE, BUT--
WHY, OF COURSE YOU MAY JOIN US! PLEASE, HAVE A SEAT.

MY SISTERS AND I ARE
ROUTE TO SEE OUR COUSINS
IDE GLASGOW. WHAT ABOUT YOU?
IS YOUR TRIP FOR BUSINESS
OR PLEASURE?
I WOULD SAY BUSINESS, BUT I ALWAYS FIND TIME FOR PLEASURE.
DID YOU EEL THAT? TRAIN SEEMS HAVE PICKED UP SPEED.
HOW ON EARTH COULD YOU FEEL SUCH A THING?
YOU ARE RIGHT, DOCTOR, I SENSE IT AS WELL. THERE IS SOMETHING WRONG WITH THIS TRAIN.
TIME TO END THIS, SISTER.
GENTLEMEN, I BELIEVE THE NEXT STOP FOR YOU BOTH...
...IS YOUR DEATH.

YOUR BEAUTY IS BEYOND COMPARE. MOST OF THE WOMEN IN MY VILLAGE ARE ROUGHER TO THE TOUCH. BUT YOU ARE SO SOFT AND SWEET.
ARE YOU SAYING INTIMACY BETWEEN WOMEN IS CUSTOMARY IN YOUR VILLAGE?
MY PEOPLE BELIEVE THAT I AM A WOMAN OF TWO SPIRITS... TO BE DRAWN TO BOTH MEN AND WOMEN IS A GIFT.
HERE IT IS CALLED DEVIANT OR MUCH WORSE. THEY BELIEVE HOMOSEXUALITY GOES AGAINST NATURE.
THOSE YOU REFER TO AS "THEY" DON'T UNDERSTAND WHAT IT FEELS LIKE TO BE FREE OF NORMAL CONSTRAINTS OF SEXUALITY. TO FLOW FROM ONE PERSON TO ANOTHER, NO MATTER THE SEX, IS MOST NATURAL.
WHAT IS IT, SEDNA? IS IT SOMETHING I SAID?
NO, I... I FEEL THERE IS EVIL ON THIS TRAIN. HURRY, LET'S GET DRESSED FOR I FEAR THIS NIGHT IS ABOUT TO TURN.
BOOOOM

SLICE HIS THROAT, SISTER. I WANT TO BATHE IN HIS BLOOD!
FRANKENSTEIN, WATCH OUT!
SMASH
LOOKS LIKE YOU COULD USE A DRINK!
GGRRR

WHAM
ARE YOU ALL RIGHT?
I'M FINE! NOW TURN INTO THE WOLF AND KILL THIS BITCH!
I HAVE A SILVER DOG COLLAR FOR THAT PRETTY NECK OF YOURS!
LOOKS LIKE THAT SILVER IS CAUSING QUITE THE REACTION!
FSHH

I DON'T NEED A KNIFE – I'LL RIP YOUR GUTS OUT WITH MY BARE HANDS!
KRUSH
FUCK YOU!
NOW, THAT'S NOT HOW YOU SHOULD SPEAK TO A LADY!
SISTER, USE THE CHAIN!

YOU ARE BEAUTIFUL. SO SAD THAT I AM GOING TO RIP YOUR HEART OUT AND FEED IT TO MY SISTERS...
I HOPE THEY CHOKE ON IT AND DIE.
THANKS, LOVE.
TIME FOR YOUR CURTAIN CALL.
LET ME GET THIS OFF OF YOU, DEAR. I DESPISE SILVER AS WELL.

LOOKS LIKE YOU BOYS NEED SOME HELP.
HOMP
FFSSS

CHOOSE YOUR FINAL RESTING PLACE, THE CLIFF OR THE MOUNTAIN.

LL LEAVE
OU TO IT.
SPLUT
THIS IS WHY I HATE WEARING DRESSES, NOT PRACTICAL.
LET HIM GO, WITCH!
YOU ARE TOO LATE, FOR THE FINAL RECKONING IS UPON US. YOU WILL ALL DIE!!!

THOOM
VRIIIIIIIIII
FRANKENSTEIN, GRAB ON TO SOMETHING!
FRANKENSTEIN!!!
VROOOOOOO

DAMN THIS ENDLESS FALLING ASH. GOING TO GET THE BLACK LUNG IF WE STAND OUT HERE MUCH LONGER.
MY MISSUS SAYS MORE THAN TEN THOUSAND PEOPLE HAVE DIED FROM THE FOUL AIR. AND THAT'S ONLY IN LONDON.
WELL, WE BEST HURRY UP AND PULL IN THIS LAST LOAD BEFORE WE BECOME TEN THOUSAND AND TWO.
OH, BLOODY HELL, WE GOT ANOTHER DEAD BODY IN THE NET!
SECOND ONE THIS WEEK!
GET LAURENCE OUT HERE TO HELP WITH THIS ONE. *LAURENCE!*
FOR FUCK'S SAKE, LAURENCE! GET YOUR PALE ARSE OUT HERE... *NOW!*
SORRY, SIR. WHAT IS IT THAT YOU NEED?
'BOUT TIME YOU GET YOUR FACE OUT YER BOOKS AND COME HELP. WE GOT ANOTHER DEAD BODY. GET IT UNTANGLED AND OFF OUR BOAT... NOW.
YES, SIR.
AND HURRY UP, WOULD YA?
YES, SIR. RIGHT AWAY, SIR. IT APPEARS TO BE THE BODY OF A MAN--
--AND HE'S ALIVE!

DOCTOR FRANKENSTEIN? WHERE ARE YOU? HELLO?
NO DOCTOR HERE, LOVE. JUST YOU AND ME.
AAAAAA
YOU WITCHES NEVER SEEM TO JUST DIE *EASILY*. I FIND IT ALL VERY FRUSTRATING.
YOU TALK TOO MUCH... LET ME TAKE CARE OF THAT BY SLICING OFF YOUR HEAD.
AND HERE I THOUGHT THERE WAS A CHANCE WE'D BE FRIENDS.
NICE TRY, DEAR, BUT YOU ARE *NOT* GETTING OUT OF THIS ONE.

EY CALL YOU
, IS IT? LOOKS
KE YOUR NINE
IVES ARE UP.
SEDNA, IT'S ME... CAT. PLEASE, I AM YOUR FRIEND, DON'T HURT ME!

YOU SAVED MY LIFE! HOW CAN I EVER THANK YOU?
I HATE FOR YOU TO SEE ME THAT WAY. I'M A... *MONSTER*.
YOU ARE NO MONSTER, SEDNA. YOU ARE A BEAUTIFUL WOMAN WITH A STRONG HEART. PERHAPS WHEN THIS IS ALL OVER, THERE IS A LIFE FOR YOU AND ME TO SHARE.
I WOULD LOVE THAT VERY MUCH. BUT FIRST WE MUST FIND FRANKENSTEIN AND KILL THE OTHER WITCH.
DON'T WORRY, I ALREADY TOOK CARE OF THE OTHER WITCH.
APPEARS SHE'S HEADED FOR AN ICY GRAVE.
HAVE YOU SEEN THE DOCTOR?
NOT SINCE THE TRAIN FLIPPED OVER. WE ARE ALL LUCKY THOUGH -- AT LEAST WE DIDN'T SLIDE OFF THAT CLIFF.
OH NO... THE CLIFF!

FRANKENSTEIN?!
FRANKENSTEIN?!
FRANKENSTEIN?!
THE LAST THING I REMEMBER WAS HIM FALLING BACK TOWARDS THE CLIFF. I WILL NOT FORGIVE MYSELF IF ANYTHING--
DO *NOT* DO THAT, CAT. WE KNOW NOTHING YET SO WE MUST HOLD OUT HOPE.
YOU LOOKING FOR SOMEONE?
I THINK I SAW A MAN DOWN THERE. I BELIEVE HE'S ALIVE, BUT I SURE BET IT'S NOT FOR VERY LONG.
DOCTOR FRANKENSTEIN! HOLD TIGHT, WE'RE COMING FOR YOU!
I GOT SOME ROPE IN MY CART, LET ME FETCH IT.

ALMOST THERE, JUST HOLD TIGHT DOCTOR.
I THOUGHT WE LOST YOU, DOC. WE HAVE TO STOP WITH THESE NEAR-DEATH SCARES. MY HEART CAN'T TAKE MUCH MORE.
YOUR HEART? TRY HANGING ONTO THE SIDE OF A CLIFF WITH JUST A KNIFE! BELIEVE ME, I AM DONE WITH CHEATING DEATH!
HOW DID YOU SURVIVE THAT FALL?
IT WAS THIS KNIFE THAT LILY GAVE ME BEFORE WE DEPARTED. SHE SAID IT WOULD PROTECT US, THAT IT WAS BLESSED BY THE HOLY ORDER. NEVER THOUGHT IT WOULD SAVE ME FROM A THOUSAND-FOOT FALL.
THE GODS WERE SMILING ON YOU, DOCTOR.
DOES THIS MEAN YOU'VE FOUND FAITH?
THERE WAS A TIME WHEN I THOUGHT I ACTUALLY WAS A GOD... THAT HAS SINCE PASSED. FOR NOW, I WILL CALL WHAT JUST HAPPENED A MIRACLE AND LEAVE IT AT THAT.
YOU SURE ARE AN ODD BUNCH. WHERE YOU HEADED?
WE ARE ON OUR WAY TO THE TOWN OF CHAILL. DO YOU KNOW HO FAR AWAY IT IS? OR IF HE WILL BE ARRIVING SOON
THERE BE NO HELP COMIN' FOR HOURS. BUT I CAN TAKE YOU TO CHAILL... FOR A PRICE.
WE HAVE THE MONEY AND WOULD APPRECIATE A RIDE. BUT WERE YOU NOT A PASSENGER ON THE TRAIN?
I'M NOT SO FANCY LIKE YOU LORDS AND LADIES. I WAS NEARBY AND SAW IT ALL HAPPEN. THOUGHT NICE PEOPLE LIKE YOU MIGHT NEED SOME HELP. COME ON, MY WAGON BE RIGHT OVER THERE.

WAKE UP, MISS LILY.
ETHAN, IS THAT YOU?
ETHAN IS GONE, MY LITTLE WATER LILY. LEFT YOU THE MOMENT HE WOKE FROM HIS SLUMBER. I FOUND YOU ON THE FLOOR, LIKE A SHUNNED, ABANDONED PUPPY. YOU POOR, POOR LITTLE THING.
LORD HYDE, WHAT HAVE YOU DONE? UNDO THESE CHAINS AT ONCE! YOU CAN'T DO THIS TO ME, YOU BASTARD!
I'M NOT THE VILLAIN IN THIS TALE. YOUR BOYFRIEND RAN OUT ON YOU, PERHAPS HE DESIRES A WOMAN WITH AN ACTUAL BEATING HEART.
I DON'T UNDERSTAND WHAT YOU ARE IMPLYING.
YOU'RE SMART ENOUGH, YOU KNOW DAMN WELL WHAT I MEAN. YOU'RE A DEAD GIRL, AREN'T YOU, MISS LILY? YOUR HEART DOES NOT BEAT AND...
YOUR SKIN IS ICE COLD TO THE TOUCH. YOU DIED, BUT BY SOME MIRACLE YOU HAVE BEEN REBORN. YOU SEE, I TOO HAVE BEEN REBORN. THOUGH I DID NOT DIE, PER SE, I HAVE COME INTO A BRAND-NEW LIFE. WHAT ONCE WAS A MOTH NOW STANDS A BEAUTIFUL BUTTERFLY.
YOU ARE NO BUTTERFLY. MONSTROUS IS MORE LIKE IT. NOW LET ME GO BEFORE I--
BEFORE YOU WHAT, TRY TO HURT ME? I AM ALL-POWERFUL NOW. I HAVE THE BLOOD OF THE DEVIL RUNNING THROUGH MY VEINS. SOON YOU WILL KNEEL TO ME.
I KNEEL TO NO MAN.
HA! A WOMAN LIKE YOU, ONE WHO SLEEPS ROUGH? I BET YOU KNEEL TO MANY MEN.

YOU THINK YOU KNOW ME? YOU THINK BECAUSE I AM A WOMAN YOU CAN LOCK ME UP AND EXPECT ME TO DO AS YOU PLEASE? YOU'RE NOTHING BUT A BRUTE, A MONSTER, AND A *FREAK*. LET ME GO BEFORE I BREAK THESE CHAINS AND RIP YOU APART. YOU WILL THEN LEARN TO NEVER FUCK WITH A WOMAN LIKE ME EVER AGAIN.
I LIKE YOU. YOU ARE UNLIKE ANY OTHER WOMAN. YOU SEE, THIS NEW POWER I POSSESS IS STILL LIMITING I NEED ONE LAST ELEMENT FOR MY FORMULA. YOU ARE UND THAT WALKS, TALKS, AND PROBABLY FUCKS AS IF YOU AR ALIVE. YOUR IMMORTALITY IS *EXACTLY* WHAT I NEED.
TAKE THAT NEEDLE OUT OF ME AT ONCE!
NOT BEFORE I GET SOME OF THAT LIVING-DEAD BLOOD THAT RUNS THROUGH YOU...
FINALLY, IMMORTALITY. NOW I WILL BE GOD.
YOU FOOLISH DOG, GO FIND A BONE TO CHEW BEFORE I BREAK YOU IN HALF.
CHAC

SNAP
YOU ARE NO MATCH FOR ME, WOLF MAN. TIME TO DIE.
KRUSH
HOPE YOU SUFFER AS
E LAST FEW REMAINING
ATHS LEAVE YOUR BODY.
TIME FOR YOU TO DIE.
YOU STUPID GIRL, NOTHING WILL KILL ME NOW.
LILY, GO FIND ETHAN. I WILL HANDLE THIS BEAST. GO!

IN THE 16TH CENTURY THAT IS WHERE FATHER JOHN GERALD WAS HUNG. THE ENGLISH GOVERNMENT FOUND HIM GUILTY AND HELD HIM PRISONER BECAUSE HE WAS SECRETLY SPREADING CATHOLICISM IN LONDON.
AND THEY CALL ME A MONSTER.
HE ESCAPED, CONTINUED SPREADING THE WORD OF GOD UNTIL HE DIED IN HIS SEVENTIES. IT'S THE POWER OF PRAYER. I PRAYED THAT ONE DAY YOU AND I WOULD BE TOGETHER.
AND HERE WE STAND WITH OUR BABY ARRIVING ANY MOMENT. WE ARE MASTER OF OUR UNIVERSE. A FAMILY T RULE THEM ALL. COME, THE MO IS FULL TONIGHT. IT IS TIME TO MEET OUR CHILD.
I JUST NEED ONE MORE MOMENT ALONE.
AS YOU WISH.

ETHAN, I BELIEVE THERE A PART OF YOU THAT CAN FEEL PRESENCE. TAP INTO THAT NOW, YOU MUST HEAR ME. THAT IS NOT VANESSA IVES... SHE IS GONE FROM THIS WORLD.
THAT WOMAN WHO CARRIES YOUR CHILD IS THE FATHER OF *LIES*. SHE IS THE *DEVIL*, PULLING YOU TOWARD DARKNESS. FIND THE LIGHT, ETHAN. FIND THE TRUTH. PLEASE GOD, LET HIM HEAR ME!
MALCOLM?
YES, I AM HERE FOR YOU, MY SON. YOU CAN'T SEE ME, BUT LISTEN TO MY WORDS.
NO, IT CAN'T BE. YOUR VOICE... IT'S INSIDE MY HEAD. AM I BEING TRICKED?
THERE'S NO TRICKERY, I AM WITH YOU. BELIEVE ME, THE VANESSA THAT IS HERE WILL LEAD YOU INTO TEMPTATION AND DESTROY YOU AND ALL MANKIND. YOU MUST NOT LET THAT HAPPEN. YOU MUST *STOP* HER.
THIS VOICE IS ***NOT*** SIR MALCOLM. IT IS A LIE, TRYING TO TEMPT ME AWAY FROM MY LOVE AND OUR BABY. LEAVE ME ***BE,*** CRUEL VOICE. I MUST BE WITH MY CHILD.
HEED MY WARNING, ETHAN -- FOR IF YOU BRING THAT CHILD INTO THIS WORLD, MANKIND WILL CEASE TO EXIST. YOU MUST DESTROY THE CHILD... AND SATAN.

WE APPRECIATE THE HELP, KID, BUT ARE YOU SURE THIS IS THE RIGHT WAY? BEEN AT IT FOR HOURS.
I BE TAKIN' YOU TO THE RIGHT SPOT, JUST AROUND THIS BEND. YOU TRUST ME?
YES, WE HAVE ALL THE TRUST IN THE WORLD. JUST A BIT EXHAUSTED AND THIRSTY.
THIRSTY, YOU SAY? I KNOW THE PERFECT PLACE. NOT FAR NOW. JUST RIGHT ROUND THIS CORNER, SEE.
DIDN'T I SAY I'D LEAD YE TO THE RIGHT PLACE. HERE BE THE TOWN OF CHAILL.
APPEARS THAT THERE IS NOT A SOUL AROUND. ARE YOU SURE THIS IS THE RIGHT PLACE?
YES, COME, COME. EVERYONE'LL BE AT THE PUB 'BOUT NOW, *KING BILLY'S.* WELL TIDY SCRAN THEY HAVE... BEST MINCE AND TATTIES IN ALL SCOTLAND.
COULD SURE USE A DRINK. OKAY, KID, TAKE US TO *KING BILLY'S.*
WELL, HERE YE ARE. BEST KEEP TO YE SELVES, NOT THE FRIENDLIEST OF FOLKS.
THANK YOU, NOW HERE'S A FEW BOB FOR YOUR TROUBLE. GO ON, SKEDADDLE OFF.
PERHAPS WE SHOULD ASK SOME OF THE LOCALS HOW TO GET TO THE ISLAND OF MARDH BEO?
BEFORE WE DO THAT, WHO WANTS A PINT? ON ME.

YOU BROUGHT THEM RIGHT TO US. YOU HAVE DONE WELL.
HAND OVER THE COINS AND PROMISE NOT TO HURT THEM TOO BADLY... THEY ARE NICE ENOUGH FOLK.
Billy's
THE BOY WAS RIGHT, NOT THE FRIENDLIEST GROUP OF PEOPLE.
IT'S THE WEATHER. WHEN YOU RARELY SEE THE SUN, IT WILL MAKE ANYONE A BIT SURLY. WHY DO YOU THINK I MOVED TO LONDON?
COME ON NOW, WHAT D'YOU WANT?
WE'LL TAKE FOUR PINTS--
AND DIRECTIONS TO THE ISLAND OF MARDH BEO.
WHY ARE YOU BLATHERING ON OUT MARDH BEO? NO ONE EVER AKS OF THAT DEAD PLACE, UNLESS YOU WANT TO DIE YERSELVES.
WE MEAN NO DISRESPECT. IT IS A MATTER OF UPMOST IMPORTANCE THAT WE GET TO THE ISLAND. IF ANYONE CAN PROVIDE US PASSAGE, IT WOULD BE GREATLY APPRECIATED.
AYE, RIGHT, YOU FANCY ENGLISH ARE NOT'IN' BUT TROUBLE -- COMING HERE, STICKING YOUR NOSES WHERE THEY DON'T BELONG. I OUGHT TO STRIKE YOU DOWN RIGHT HERE, BEFORE YOU--
THAT'S ENOUGH FROM YOU, BOYS. LEAVE THE NICE ENGLISHMEN ALONE. I'LL HANDLE IT FROM HERE. COME, JOIN ME.
THE NAME'S QUINCEY MORRIS, AND I CAN TAKE YOU TO THAT BLOODY ISLAND.

IT'S TIME MY LOVE. LET US WELCOME OUR FUTURE KING TOGETHER.
WHAT DO YOU REQUIRE OF US, MASTER?
CUT IT OUT OF ME, NOW!

TELL US, MR. MORRIS, WHAT DOES AN AMERICAN WAY THE HELL OUT HERE KNOW ABOUT MARDH BEO?
THE ISLAND OF THE DEAD? PLEASE, DARLING, OVER MY MANY YEARS ABROAD I'VE COME TO KNOW ABOUT ALL THINGS DEAD AND DYING.
THEN YOU AND MISS HARTDEGEN HAVE A LOT IN COMMON. SO, CAN YOU TAKE US TO THE ISLAND?
FIRST, WHY DO YOU WANT TO GO THERE? ASK ANYONE IN THIS PUB AND THEY'LL TELL YOU THAT THOSE WHO TRAVEL TO THE ISLAND NEVER RETURN. WHAT MAKES YOU THINK YOU'RE ANY DIFFERENT?
WE HAVE NO CHOICE, IT IS LIFE AND DEATH. THERE IS AN ARTIFACT ON THAT ISLAND THAT WE BELIEVE CAN END THIS PERPETUAL DARKNESS AND RETURN ORDER TO THE WORLD.
SAVE THE THEATRICS FOR THE STAGE, THERE IS SOMETHING VERY REAL AND VERY DEADLY ON THE ISLAND.
AND WHAT MAKES YOU THE EXPERT?
THE LOVE OF MY LIFE, MY DEAR LUCY, WAS TAKEN FROM ME BY THE COUNT DRACULA WHO RESIDES ON THAT ROCK. I AM DESPERATE TO SEEK REVENGE FOR HER DEATH. I WANT TO SEND THE BEAST BACK TO HELL WHERE HE CAME FROM. BUT HE'S PROTECTED BY HIS ARMY OF UNDEAD, AND THEY'RE TOO POWERFUL FOR ME TO TAKE ON MY OWN.
THAN WE MAKE A DEAL, YOU GET US TO THE ISLAND, AND WE WILL HELP SEEK YOUR REVENGE.
I JUST MET YOU, HOW AM I SUPPOSED TO BELIEVE YOU FOUR CAN TAKE ON SUCH POWERFUL EVIL?
ALL OF US HAVE FACED DOWN EVIL MANY TIMES AND DESTROYED IT WITH OUR CLAWS AND TEETH. LET'S NOT WASTE ANOTHER SECOND.
I LIKE YOUR MOXIE, DARLING. PERHAPS YOU ARE THE ONES I NEED FOR SUCH AN ENDEAVOR. HELL, I BEEN SITTING HERE FOR WEEKS AND NO ONE HAS TAKEN UP THE OFFER.

MR. MORRIS, I THOUGHT YOU SAID WE DON'T REQUIRE A BOAT? HOW ARE YOU PLANNING FOR US TO CROSS?
TRUST ME, THERE IS A BOAT.
YOU JUST HAVE TO KNOW HOW TO CALL THE FERRYMAN.
WE WILL NEED TO OFFER A TOLL FOR PASSAGE.
LIKE A FEW POUNDS? I THINK I HAVE--
MORE THAN A FEW POUNDS. HE REQUIRES BIGGER PRIZE... LIKE ONE OF OUR SOULS.

GOOD TO SEE YOU, KHARON. IT'S BEEN A WHILE. WOULD OU PLEASE TAKE MY FRIENDS AND ME TO THE ISLAND? WE'RE IN A BIT OF A RUSH SO IF YOU WOULDN'T MIND--
YOU MUST PAY THE TOLL.
YOU'RE ALWAYS SO DEMANDING. WHY DON'T WE SETTLE UP THE PAYMENT ONCE YOU GET US ACROSS? WE'RE GOOD FOR IT, I PROMISE.
YOU MUST PAY THE TOLL! I NEED YOUR SOUL.
LOOK, PAL, YOU HAVE TO BE REASONABLE. NONE OF US CAME HERE ON A SUICIDE MISSION, SO CAN YOU JUST WORK WITH US A BIT?
HERE, I GIVE YOU THIS SACRED KNIFE BLESSED BY THE HOLY ORDER. IT'S ONE OF A KIND.
DOCTOR ARE YOU MAD? YOU SAID WE NEEDED THAT KNIFE WHEN FACING DRACULA! HOW ARE YOU PLANNING TO DEFEAT HIM WITHOUT IT?
WE'LL FIND ANOTHER WAY.
THIS WILL DO FOR A ONE WAY PASSAGE. COME.

YOU ALL MUST PROMISE NOT TO STARE INTO THE WATER. THERE ARE NYMPHS EVERYWHERE SERVING AS GUARDIANS OF DRACULA'S LAIR. DON'T BE TEMPTED BY THEIR BEAUTY, THEY ARE VICIOUS CREATURES THAT WILL RIP YOUR SKIN RIGHT OFF. ONE LOOK INTO THEIR EYES IS ALL IT TAKES. TRUST ME, I LEARNED MY LESSON ONCE.
YOU SEEM TO KNOW MUCH ABOUT DRACULA AND THIS ISLAND. HOW ARE WE TO BELIEVE THIS IS NOT A TRAP?
BECAUSE THE WOMAN I LOVE MORE THAN ANYTHING IN THIS WORLD WAS KILLED BY THAT FANG-TOOTHED BEAST. I'VE BEEN TO THE ISLAND AND BARELY ESCAPED WITH MY LIFE. I PREPARED, LEARNING EVERYTHING I COULD ABOUT DRACULA AND HIS DEMON FAMILIARS.
BUT I COULD NOT TAKE HIM DOWN ALONE, I NEEDED TO FIND OTHERS WHO ARE NOT AFRAID.
BEAUTIFUL.
NANUQ! DO NOT LOOK INTO THE WATER OR YOU--

NANUQ, HERE, GRAB ONTO MY HAND!
GOD DAMN IT... WHY CAN'T YOU PEOPLE LISTEN TO ME? I KNOW WHAT I'M TALKING ABOUT WHEN IT COMES TO THIS PLACE!
GRRRR
LORD HAVE MERCY.
THACK
BAM! BAM! BAM!
DARLING, THAT SURE IS A UNIQUE TALENT YOU HAVE. GOOD TO KNOW WE'VE GOT A WEREWOLF ON OUR SIDE.
TWO... I AM ONE AS WELL.
WELL ,THAT CHANGES EVERYTHING, NOW, DOESN'T IT? OKAY, LET'S GO BEFORE WE GET INTO ANY MORE TROUBLE. WE SHOULD BE GETTING CLOSE.

TOC
TOC

OUR MASTER AS BEEN EXPECTING YOU FOR SOME TIME.
OW DID HE OW WE WERE COMING?
THE COUNT KNOWS EVERYTHING. HE HAS PREPARED A FEAST FOR YOU. COME, LET ME SHOW YOU TO THE DINING ROOM.
MR. MORRIS, THIS DOESN'T FEEL RIGHT.
TRUST ME, DOC, THIS IS GOING EXACTLY AS I PLANNED. JUST FOLLOW MY LEAD.
WELCOME, EVERYONE. I HAVE BEEN ANTICIPATING YOUR ARRIVAL. I HOPE IT WASN'T TOO DIFFICULT GETTING HERE.
RAN INTO A BIT OF TROUBLE ON THE LAKE. YOU MIGHT HAVE TO REPLACE SOME OF YOUR NYMPHS. SORRY ABOUT THAT.
WELL... REGARDLESS, I WANT TO THANK YOU, MR. MORRIS. YOU HAVE DONE WHAT I ASKED, LEADING THIS GROUP SAFELY TO ME. PLEASE HAVE A SEAT, EVERYONE, AND LET US EAT. I'M SURE YOU ARE ALL PLENTY HUNGRY.
WE DIDN'T COME HERE TO DINE. WHAT THE HELL IS GOING ON HERE, QUINCEY?
YOU ASKED FOR MY HELP IN GETTING HERE, AND I FOLLOWED THROUGH WITH MY PROMISE.
YOU SET US UP!
AND WHAT DO YOU GET OUT OF ALL THIS?

QUINCEY... YOU'VE COME FOR ME, MY LOVE.
MY DARLING LUCY, I'M HERE.
YOU LIED TO US. WHY?
THE COUNT PROMISED ME I COULD BE WITH MY LUCY AS LONG AS I BROUGHT YOU HERE IN ONE PIECE.
YOU WILL PAY FOR THIS.
I STRONGLY SUGGEST YOU NOT TURN INTO A WOLF, DEAR. I KNOW WHAT YOU ARE AND HOW TO STOP YOU. YOU MOVE ANY CLOSER AND YOU GET A SILVER BULLET TO THE CHEST.
NOW HOLD IT RIGHT THERE, MR. MORRIS. I ASKED FOR ABSOLUTELY NO VIOLENCE IN MY HOME. PUT THE GUN DOWN AND LET'S HAVE A CIVIL DISCUSSION WITH DOCTOR FRANKENSTEIN AND MISS HARTDEGEN.
SEDNA, NO!
BAM

WHAAAAAHHH!!!!
MASTER SATAN, YOU HAVE A BEAUTIFUL BABY DAUGHTER.
LOOK AT HER, ETHAN. SHE IS THE EW LEADER OF THIS RTH, OUR BEAUTIFUL LORD AND SAVIOR. THE ENTIRE WORLD WILL CALL HER JEZEBEL.
WE ARE FINALLY A FAMILY.
MASTER, EXCUSE ME FOR INTERRUPTING BUT--
WHAT IS IT? SPEAK, WITCH!
THERE'S ANOTHER?
ANOTHER, WHAT?
YOU ARE ABOUT TO GIVE BIRTH TO ANOTHER CHILD. A TWIN.

SEDNA, MY LOVE, PLEASE DO NOT DIE ON ME. HOLD TIGHT.
CAT... I AM SO SORRY... I LOVE...
QUINCEY HOW COULD YOU? WE TRUSTED YOU.
YOU'D DO THE SAME THING FOR THE ONE YOU LOVE. NOW TELL YOUR ATTACK DOG TO STAND DOWN OR HE'LL BE LYING ON THE FLOOR NEXT TO HIS SISTER WITH ONE PULL OF THE TRIGGER.
THAT'S ENOUGH!
I SWEAR TO GOD I'LL PUT SILVER BULLET R IN THAT FURR FACE OF HIS
I SAID ENOUGH!
ONE MORE OUTBURST AND I WILL SEND YOU ALL TO THE DUNGEON AND ALLOW MY FAMILIARS TO FEAST UPON YOUR BODIES. I HAVE FINALLY FOUND PEACE HERE AND WILL NOT ALLOW IT TO BE DISTURBED.
NO, PUT HER DOWN. WHERE ARE YOU TAKING MY SISTER?
NANUQ, GO AND LOOK AFTER YOUR SISTER. WE'LL BE FINE HERE.
MY FAMILIARS WILL DO ALL THEY CAN TO SAVE HER LIFE. YOU MUST TRUST ME.
AS FOR YOU, MR. MORRIS...YOU AND MISS LUCY ARE FREE TO GO. LEAVE NOW BEFORE I CHANGE MY MIND.
THANK YOU FOR KEEPING YOUR WORD. COME LUCY, LET'S GET THE HELL OUT OF HERE.

BUT QUINCEY, THOUGHT WE WERE GOING TO FIND A CURE FOR ME.
SHHH... WE WILL FIND IT ANOTHER WAY. THEN WE WILL SEEK OUR REVENGE. COME NOW, DEAR.
MISS HARTDEGEN, DR. FRANKENSTEIN...PLEASE FOLLOW ME.
HOW DO WE KNOW WE CAN TRUST YOU? LAST TIME WE WERE FACE-TO-FACE YOU HAD YOUR FAMILIARS TRY TO EXTERMINATE US. TOO BAD YOU LOST.
AND IT WAS YOU WHO TOOK MISS IVES. YOU ARE THE REASON SHE IS DEAD.
YES, YOU ARE BOTH CORRECT. I LOVED MISS IVES MORE THAN ANYTHING ON THIS EARTH. BUT IT WAS MY DESIRE AND GREED THAT LEAD TO HER DEATH AND FOR THAT I AM DEEPLY SORRY. BUT NOW THERE IS A GREATER EVIL OUT IN THE WORLD. THAT IS THE REASON YOU ARE HERE. PLEASE COME WITH ME...THERE'S LITTLE TIME.
HOW DO YOU KNOW WHY WE'RE HERE?
I HAVE BEEN WATCHING YOU... NOW PLEASE WE MUST--
UGH...
COUNT DRACULA, ARE YOU ALRIGHT? WHAT'S WRONG?
IT'S HAPPENING...
WHAT? WHAT IS HAPPENING?
THE CHILDREN HAVE BEEN BORN.
CHILDREN?

TWINS. LUCIFER HAS CREATED HIS OWN BODY AND BLOOD ON THIS EARTH. LIFE AS WE KNOW IT WILL SOON BE OVER. I BELIEVE THAT IS WHY YOU HAVE COME.
THE SABLE FLAME. THE PROPHECY SAYS THAT IT IS THE ONLY WEAPON POWERFUL ENOUGH TO SEND LUCIFER BACK TO HELL.
IS THAT TRUE?
YES. AND IT IS YOURS.
BUT THIS MAKES NO SENSE. WHY ARE YOU SO WILLING TO HELP US NOW, WHEN ALL YOU WANTED TO DO WAS DESTROY MANKIND?
OUR GOALS ARE ONE AND THE SAME. FOR I WANT TO DESTROY MY BROTHER JUST AS BADLY AS YOU DO. THUS, WE ARE BONDED IN BLOOD.
AND I THOUGHT THE RIVALRY BETWEEN MY BROTHERS WAS ROUGH.
LUCIFER ISN'T SIMPLY MY BROTHER, WE ARE TWINS...TWO SIDES OF THE SAME COIN. NONE THE LESS, HE MUST BE DESTROYED. THAT IS WHY I BROUGHT YOU BOTH HERE. I HAVE BEEN WITH YOU ALL THIS TIME, LEADING YOU TO ME.
"I WATCHED AS YOU FOUGHT OFF THE ARMY AT THE CHURCH.
"I CONVINCED THE YOUNG LAD TO BRING YOU TO MR. MORRIS.
"AND IT WAS I WHO STEERED YOU TO THIS ISLAND."

BELIEVE THIS IS EEP IT SAFE, YOU MIGHT AVE NEED FOR IT.
WHY THIS? ROPHECY THAT THE LAME WILL ATAN BACK ELL. WHY US HERE HE WEAPON TROY YOUR HER HAS IN YOUR SSION ALL ONG?
BECAUSE ONLY THE LIVING MAY WIELD ITS POWER. YOU HUMANS DON'T QUITE UNDERSTAND THE FULL SCOPE OF WHAT YOU ARE IN THE MIDDLE OF. LET ME TELL YOU THE REAL STORY.
"BEFORE MY BROTHER RULED THE UNDERWORLD, THERE WAS ANOTHER IN POWER. HER NAME WAS LILITH. SHE WAS THE GODDESS OF HELL WHOSE SOLE DESIRE WAS TO BECOME HUMAN. SHE MADE A DEAL WITH YOUR GOD; SHE COULD BECOME HUMAN ONLY IF SHE FOUND SOMEONE TO REPLACE HER IN HELL.
"GOD MADE HER INTO THE MOST BEAUTIFUL WOMAN ON EARTH AND GAVE HER THE WEAPON THAT COULD SEND THE ONE SHE CHOSE INTO HELL FOREVER. HAVING JUST EXPELLED MY BROTHER AND ME FROM HIS HEAVENLY REALM, GOD PRESENTED US, HIS FALLEN ANGELS, AS HER POTENTIAL PROXY.
"LILITH AND I FELL IN LOVE, WHICH FILLED MY BROTHER WITH JEALOUSY AND RAGE. HE TURNED ON US BOTH. THUS LILITH USED THE SABLE FLAME, SENDING LUCIFER INTO THE FIERY PIT OF HELL.
"GOD WAS FURIOUS THAT LILITH FELL IN LOVE WITH ME, SO HE TURNED HER INTO A MONSTER -- MAKING HER THE VERY FIRST VAMPIRE. SHE BLAMED ME FOR WHAT HAD BECOME OF HER, AND DID NOT WANT TO LIVE AN ETERNAL LIFE AS A CREATURE OF THE NIGHT ALONE."

BUT WE WERE TOLD THAT LILITH WAS A WARRIOR FOR GOD AND THAT THE SABLE FLAME WAS GIVEN TO HER FOR PROTECTION.
NO ONE WANTS TO BELIEVE THEIR GOD IS A VENGEFUL, VAINGLORIOUS LORD.
AND WHAT BECAME OF LILITH?
I DROVE A STAKE THROUGH HER HEART, PLACED HER BODY IN A STONE COFFIN, AND SANK IT TO THE BOTTOM OF THIS LAKE. MY VAMPIRE GUARDS NOT ONLY PROTECT THE FLAME, BUT ALSO LILITH'S WATERY GRAVE. I INSCRIBED A WARNING ON THE COFFIN...*MORS EST ILLIS APERIRE.*
"DEATH TO THOSE THAT OPEN."
LOOK AT HOW BEAUTIFUL MY GIRLS ARE. I HAVE CREATED THE TWO MOST POWERFUL WOMEN ON THIS EARTH. MY DARLING JEZEBEL AND I SHALL NAME HER--
NO, LET ME NAME HER.
SHE WILL BE CALLED REBECCA, AFTER MY MOTHER.
DO YOU SEE? BABY REBECCA HAS A MARK ON HER ARM. IT IS A SIGN OF GREATNESS.
WHAT IS HAPPENING?
IT'S THE BEGINNING OF THE END FOR ALL MANKIND. THE APOCALYPSE IS UPON US. COME. LET US WATCH THE WORLD CRUMBLE.
WE HAVE STOLEN ALL THE POWER FROM GOD. HEAVEN BURNS, AND SOON THE EARTH SHALL BE CONSUMED BY THE FLAMES. OUT OF THE ASHES, MY DAUGHTERS AND I SHALL RISE AS THE RULERS OF THIS PLACE.

HERE, MY FRIEND, LET ME GET YOU TO SOME SHELTER. IT APPEARS THE SKY IS ON FIRE, SO WE MUST MOVE LIKE THE WIND.
HEY, LAURENCE, YOU BEST BE GETTING THAT MONSTER AS FAR AWAY FROM US AS POSSIBLE! AND DON'T PLAN ON COMING BACK, NEITHER. WE DON'T NEED A FREAK LIKE YOU ON OUR BOAT.
THAT'S RIGHT. BE GONE FROM HERE, FREAK!
PAY NO ATTENTION TO THOSE FOOLS. SMELLING FISH ALL DAY HAS ROTTED THEIR BRAINS.
BOOM
THE BOAT'S ON FIRE!!!
AHHHH!!!!
HURRY, BEFORE ARE CONSUMED BY THE FLAMES AS WELL.
THEY CALL ME LAURENCE...THAT IS THE NAME I USE NOW. BEEN SO LONG SINCE I WAS CALLED BY MY GIVEN NAME THAT I DON'T EVEN REMEMBER IT ANYMORE. WHAT CAN I CALL YOU?
I...AM... BELIAL.
WELL, BELIAL, IT APPEARS THE WORLD AROUND US IS ON FIRE.
LET IT ALL BURN TO THE GROUND.
LIFE HAS DEALT YOU A CRUEL HAND LIKE IT HAS ME. OUR SWEETEST SONGS ARE THOSE THAT TELL OF THE SADDEST THOUGHTS.
I WANT VENGEANCE. EVERYTHING WAS TAKEN FROM ME. I HAVE...NOTHING.
AYE, NOTHING IS ALL THAT I HAVE AS WELL. ALL THAT I EVER LOVED WAS RIPPED AWAY FROM ME. LIKE YOU, VENGEANCE BURNS WITHIN MY HEART.
GROAN
MY FRIEND, YOU APPEAR UNWELL. WHEN THE AIR CLEARS, I WILL TAKE YOU TO SEE A DOCTOR. THERE IS ONE I SHARE A CLOSE BOND WITH...HE WILL HELP YOU.

YOU HAVE LITTLE TIME LEFT, SO TELL ME WHERE ETHAN AND LILY HAVE GONE.
NEVER!
AHHH!!!
I WOULD RATHER DIE THAN GIVE ETHAN UP TO YOU.
UNLIKE YOU, BEAST... I HAVE BEEN FORGIVEN FOR ALL MY SINS. MAY THE SPIRTS WELCOME ME HOME.
FOOLISH OLD MAN. I KNOW ANOTHER WHO WILL LEAD ME TO ETHAN!

I DEMAND THAT YOU LET ME IN TO SEE MR. CHANDLER. HE IS BEING HELD AGAINST HIS WILL.
YOU EITHER COME TO SERVE OUR MASTER, OR YOU DIE.
THE ONLY MASTER I SERVE IS GOD IN HEAVEN, NOW TAKE ME TO--
YOUR GOD IS **DEAD,** MY DEAR.
LOOK AROUND, THE WORLD IS ON FIRE AND YOUR GOD DOES NOTHING. I USED TO BE LIKE YOU, PRAYING TO OUR LORD AND SAVIOR EVERY DAY, ASKING FOR HIS LOVE AND GUIDANCE. AND WHAT DID HE GIVE ME? NOT A DAMN THING!
BUT YOU ARE A DUKE, A MAN OF GREAT POWER AND WEALTH. HOW COULD SOMEONE LIKE YOU, WHO HAS EVERYTHING, TURN YOUR BACK ON GOD TO FOLLOW SATAN AND HIS ARMY OF DARKNESS?
NO, GOD TURNED HIS BACK ON ME. I WATCHED THE LOVE OF MY LIFE, MY DEAR WIFE KATHERINE, DIE A PAINFUL DEATH FROM CHOLERA.
SHE WAS A WONDERFUL WOMAN, ALWAYS SERVING THE POOR AND NEEDY, UNTIL SHE BECAME ILL. IN THE END THERE WAS NOTHING LEFT OF HER. AND WHERE WAS YOUR GOD THEN? HE MADE A WOMAN WHO WAS WHOLLY GOOD SUFFER AND DIE.
BUT NOW THE REST OF THE WORLD IS SUFFERING AND DYING AT THE HAND OF YOUR MASTER AND YOU DO NOTHING TO STOP IT? I, TOO, HAVE WITNESSED MUCH DEATH IN MY LIFETIME, YET I STILL REMAIN LOYAL TO THE HEAVENS ABOVE. PLEASE, I CAN SEE THE PAIN IN YOUR HEART...LET US END ALL THIS. TAKE ME TO ETHAN.
ETHAN? WHY WOULD I TAKE YOU TO THE FATHER OF LUCIFER'S CHILDREN?
NO! YOU LIE!

THEY ARE A FAMILY NOW AND WILL RULE THIS WORLD TOGETHER. SATAN'S CHILDREN WERE MADE FLESH -- SO TODAY WE REJOICE.
ETHAN CANNOT BE THE FATHER OF SATAN'S CHILDREN. IT'S NOT POSSIBLE.
WHY NOT JOIN US?
I WALKED THAT PATH BEFORE, IT LED TO AN EMPTY HEART AND MIND. NEVER AGAIN.
THEN YOU SHALL DIE A PAINFUL DEATH.
YOU FOOL...WHEN YOU ARE OF THE UNDEAD LIKE ME, YOU NO LONGER FEAR DEATH.
I BELIEVE IT IS YOU WHO SHALL DIE PAINFULLY.
CHAC
STOP! COME ANY CLOSER AND I SQUEEZE THE LIFE OUT OF YOUR PRECIOUS DUKE. TAKE ME TO ETHAN CHANDLER OR HE DIES.

BLESSED DAY IS HERE, FOR NOW MY TWO QUEENS SHALL RULE AS KINGS. FAMOUS BY THEIR BIRTH, SO SHALL THEY BE BOTH FEARED AND LOVED BY ALL OF THIS EARTH.
AS I LOOK UPON OUR BEAUTIFUL DAUGHTERS' FACES... I FEEL MORE HUMAN NOW THAN EVER BEFORE. VANESSA, I DREAMED OF THE DAY WE HAD CHILDREN OF OUR OWN. THE HEAVENS HAVE GRANTED US TWO WONDERFUL GIFTS.
THE HEAVENS? DO YOU THINK GOD HAD ANYTHING TO DO WITH THE BIRTH OF MY CHILDREN? NO, I CREATED THEM.
HE COULDN'T HANDLE FREE THINKERS, AND FELT JEALOUS OF OUR RISE TO POWER, SO HE TOSSED MY BROTHER AND ME OUT LIKE PIECES OF TRASH. NOW, I HOLD ALL THE POWER. YOU MUST CHOOSE, ETHAN. STAND NEXT TO ME WITH MY CHILDREN -- OR DIE LIKE THE REST OF MANKIND.
I WILL ALWAYS BE WITH YOU, VANESSA.
I KNEW YOU'D MAKE THE RIGHT CHOICE. NOW, LET US SPEAK TO THE REST OF THE WORLD THROUGH MY FOLLOWERS.
HUMANS OF THIS EARTH. THIS IS YOUR MASTER LUCIFER SPEAKING TO YOU--

...THROUGH MY MANY FOLLOWERS. I, SATAN, HAVE COME TO PROCLAIM VICTORY. YOUR GOD HAS GIVEN UP HIS POWER SO THAT MY DAUGHTERS MAY NOW REIGN.
THEY WILL BE YOUR MASTERS NOW.
YOU ARE ALL NOW UNDER MY CONTROL -- AND WILL WATCH AS THE EARTH BURNS.
DO NOT FEAR MY DEMONS. THEY ARE MY GUARDIANS, PROTECTING ALL THOSE WHO WILL JOIN ME...
...BY REMOVING THOSE FROM THIS LAND WHO REFUSE TO FOLLOW ME.
YOU ARE ALL UNDER OUR RULE NOW. SO BOW DOWN AND ACCEPT YOUR LEADERS...

...OR PERISH IN THE PIT OF HELL.
MASTER, I AM SORRY TO INTERRUPT BUT THERE IS A BIT OF AN ISSUE WITH--
ETHAN!
HOW DARE YOU BARGE IN HERE LIKE THIS, CHAINED LIKE A DOG. WHAT HAPPENED, YOU FOOL?
THIS WOMAN... SHE...OVER-POWERED ME. SHE IS OF THE LIVING DEAD.
THEN SHE IS ONE OF MY FOLLOWERS.
NEVER! THOUGH MY BODY MAY NO LONGER BE ALIVE, I WILL NEVER FOLLOW THE PATHETIC AND WEAK SATAN.
THAT IS ENOUGH, MISS CROFT! DO NOT SPEAK THAT WAY ABOUT THE MOTHER OF MY CHILDREN.
YOUR CHILDREN? ETHAN, WHAT HAS HAPPENED? YOU'VE BEEN POSSESSED BY THIS MONSTER.
DEMONS, RIP THEIR HEADS OFF. I WANT THEM ON SPIKES OUTSIDE THE GATES TO WARN OTHERS TO NEVER BETRAY ME.
BUT MASTER, I HAVE DONE ALL THAT YOU HAVE ASKED OF ME. I HAVE RECRUITED YOUR FOLLOWERS AND EVEN KILLED FOR YOU. WHY DO THIS? PLEASE--
YOU HAVE SERVED YOUR PURPOSE, BUT I HAVE NO USE FOR SUCH IMPOTENCE.
ETHAN, PLEASE...DO SOMETHING!
I COMMAND YOU TO STOP! VANESSA, LET ME DISPENSE OF THE WOMAN ON MY OWN.
AS YOU WISH BUT DO IT QUICKLY. I WANT TO SEE HER HEAD ON A STAKE FROM MY WINDOW. GO...BUT LEAVE MY CHILDREN
DEMONS, MAKE SURE ETHAN GOES THROUGH WITH HIS ORDERS. IF HE REFUSES... THEN KILL HIM!

THE GROUND IS SHAKING!
WE ARE RUNNING OUT OF TIME! YOU MUST TAKE THE SABLE FLAME AND USE IT AGAINST SATAN AND HIS NEW BORN CHILDREN BEFORE THE WORLD PERISHES.
IT'S ALREADY TOO LATE... WE ARE HUNDREDS OF MILES FROM LONDON.
GO -- RETRIEVE THE FLAME, AND I WILL SHOW YOU A PATH. GO, NOW!
NOW, TELL US COUNT, HOW DO YOU PROPOSE WE GET BACK TO LONDON IN TIME?
THE SABLE FLAME WILL LIGHT YOUR WAY.
THE FLAME WILL PROVIDE YOU A SAFE AND SPEEDY PASSAGE. IT WILL LEAD YOU BACK TO LONDON, POST HASTE.
BUT WHAT ABOUT SEDNA AND NANUQ? WE CAN'T LEAVE WITHOUT THEM!
THERE'S NO TIME. THIS PASSAGE WILL ONLY STAY OPEN FOR MERE MOMENTS. GO NOW!
I AM NOT SURE ABOUT THIS...
"FOR WE WALK BY FAITH, NOT BY SIGHT."

MY SISTER IS *DYING.* THERE MUST BE SOMETHING YOU CAN DO.
YES, WE CAN SAVE HER. BUT SHE WON'T BE EXACTLY THE SISTER YOU KNOW. SHE WILL BE...ENHANCED.
ENHANCED? HOW SO?
THE ONLY WAY TO SAVE HER S TO MAKE HER ONE OF US. SHE WILL NEVER FEEL PAIN AGAIN -- AND WILL LIVE FOR ETERNITY.
NO -- I WILL NOT ALLOW HER TO BECOME A FREAK LIKE YOU ALL.
YOU SAY FREAK LIKE IT'S A BAD THING. LOOK AROUND, DO YOU THINK THAT IS HOW WE FEEL? YOU, TOO, COULD OIN US. YOU WILL FEEL ALL E PLEASURE AND NONE OF HE PAIN IN LIFE. YOU WILL HAVE EVERY WANT AND DESIRE FULFILLED. YOU FIND ME BEAUTIFUL, DO YOU NOT?
VERY MUCH.
YOU CAN HAVE ALL OF US IF YOU WANT. AND WE CAN HAVE ALL OF YOU.
JOIN US.
AND WE WILL LIVE FOREVER? NO PAIN, NO SUFFERING?
AND ALL YOUR HEART'S DESIRE. LET ME SHOW YOU.
FIRST, SAVE MY SISTER.
PROMISE ME SHE WILL LIVE AND I'LL DO WHATEVER YOU ASK.
YOU HAVE MY WORD. NOW, ARE YOU READY?
YES!

MY DEAR COUNT, THE WEREWOLVES ARE NOW WITH US.
GOOD, YOU HAVE DONE WELL.

IT IS ALL GOING AS YOU PLANNED. ONCE YOUR BROTHER IS SENT BACK TO THE UNDERWORLD, TH EARTH IS YOURS FOR THE TAKING. DOES THAT NOT EXCITE YOU? YOU SEEM...LOST.
FOR AS LONG AS I HAVE BEEN ON THIS EARTH, I HAVE WANTED TO SEE MY BROTHER SUFFER. AND NOW...I HAVE FINALLY SET IN MOTION HIS DEMISE, YET I FEEL...
YOU FEEL WHAT, MY LOVE?
WHAT HAVE I ***DONE?*** MY BROTHER IS TOO POWERFUL FOR THESE MORTALS. I HAVE SENT THEM TO THEIR GRAVES. NO...I WILL NOT STAND IDLY BY.
WHAT ARE YOU DOING? I THOUGHT THIS IS WHAT YOU ***WANTED.***
WE MUST HURRY AND HELP THE HUMANS. WE WILL GET AN ARMY AND MOVE AS MIST.

THIS IS BEYOND THE REALM OF POSSIBILITY. HOW ARE WE ABLE TO MOVE WITH SUCH EASE, SURROUNDED COMPLETELY BY WATER?
AFTER ALL THAT WE HAVE SEEN AND DONE, ***THIS*** YOU QUESTION? LOOK UP AHEAD -- IT APPEARS THERE'S AN OPENING. LET'S GO.

OH, ETHAN, ALL LIFE AS WE KNOW IT WILL CEASE TO EXIST! HOW COULD YOU?
I DID IT FOR LOVE.
FOR THE LOVE OF MISS IVES? THE WOMAN IN THAT TOWER IS NOT VANESSA. YOU MUST BELIEVE ME. SHE IS THE DEVIL, HIDING IN THE BODY OF THE WOMAN YOU ONCE LOVED.
BUT THE WOMAN WHO STANDS BEFORE YOU LOVES YOU NOW AND FOREVER.
JOIN ME, AND WE CAN END THIS DEATH AND DESTRUCTION. ***PLEASE,*** ETHAN, YOU MUST BELIEVE ME.
FFFWWWWWWW
DEAR GOD, HELL HAS TAKEN OVER THE EARTH. I FEAR WE MIGHT BE OUT OF TIME.
LOOK... UP THERE! IT'S ETHAN.
ETHAN! WE HAVE THE SABLE FLAME. WE CAN STOP ALL OF THIS.
DEMONS, KILL THOSE TWO.
NO, ETHAN! THEY ARE ON OUR SIDE.

THE SABLE FLAME. DEMONS, KILL THEM ALL. I WANT YOU TO TAKE THAT TORCH AS FAR FROM HERE AS YOU CAN. GO, DO AS I SAY!
CAT, I BELIEVE WE ARE OUTNUMBERED. WHAT DO WE DO?
WE FIGHT!
CAT, USE THE FLAME. SEND THESE DEMONS BACK TO HELL WHERE THEY BELONG!
DOCTOR, HERE, CATCH!
THERE'S JUST TOO MAN OF THEM.

ETHAN, YOU MUST STOP THIS! THESE ARE YOUR FRIENDS -- WHO WILL BE SLAUGHTERED IF YOU DON'T DO SOMETHING. PLEASE. WHY WON'T YOU LISTEN TO ME?
CHACK
ETHAN, STOP THIS! YOUR FAMILY NEEDS YOU. YOU MUST SAVE THEM FROM THIS EVIL. BE TRUE!
BE TRUE.
KRACK
SIR MALCOLM, IS THAT YOU?
YES, MY SON. I AM WITH YOU. THERE IS GOODNESS IN YOUR HEART. YOU MUST USE THE LIGHT INSIDE OF YOU TO DESTROY THIS DARKNESS. SAVE THE ONES YOU LOVE.

KRASH
MY LOVE, WHY MUST YOU BETRAY ME?
VANESSA.
YES, DEAR. YOU MUST DO SOMETHING FOR ME. TAKE THIS TORCH AND THROW IT IN THE WATER. DO IT NOW.
DON'T LISTEN TO HER, ETHAN. THAT FLAME IS THE ONLY WEAPON THAT CAN DESTROY HER ONCE AND FOR ALL. USE IT!
THERE'S THE FACE OF THE MAN I LOVE. NOW, TAKE THE FLAME AWAY FROM HERE.
YOU ARE NOT VANESSA IVES. YOU HAVE TRICKED ME TIME AND TIME AGAIN. YOU MIGHT BE IN VANESSA'S BODY -- BUT YOU DO NOT POSSESS HER SOUL.
ETHAN, I PROMISE YOU THAT I AM VANESSA. LET ME PROVE IT TO YOU WITH A KISS.
SHE'S KILLING ETHAN!
STOP, BROTHER... THIS WILL NEVER BE YOUR WORLD.
I CAN NO LONGER SIT BACK AND WATCH YOU DESTROY THIS EARTH.

ETHAN, USE THIS.
YOU WILL NEVER BE THE WOMAN VANESSA WAS. GO TO HELL, YOU BITCH.
CHAC
LET THEM GO. THIS IS BETWEEN YOU AND ME, BROTHER. TURN AND FACE ME.
COME WITH ME, LILY. WE MUST KILL SATAN'S CHILDREN BEFORE THEY CAN CAUSE ANY MORE DAMAGE.
NO, I WILL NOT LET YOU HURT THOSE BABIES. YOU TOUCH EITHER OF THEM AND I WILL END YOU.

OH, DEAR BROTHER, DRINKER OF BLOOD. YOU HAVE NO POWER HERE ANY LONGER. GO BACK TO THE CAVE WHERE YOU AND THE REST OF YOUR RODENTS SLEEP.
THIS KINGDOM COULD HAVE BEEN OURS. WE COULD HAVE RULED TOGETHER. BUT YOU TURNED YOUR BACK ON ME, YOUR OWN TWIN.
YOU WERE ALWAYS THE WEAK ONE, FUELED ONLY BY EMOTION. YOU TRIED TO TAKE OVER THIS WORLD AND FAILED. NOW IT'S MY TURN.
BUT WHY NOT *TOGETHER?* THIS IS OUR CHANCE TO BEGIN ANEW. PLEASE BROTHER, CONSIDER WHAT WE COULD DO AS ONE.
I DON'T *NEED* YOU, I HAVE MY CHILDREN TO RULE. THEY ARE MADE OF FLESH AND BLOOD AND DON'T REQUIRE DRINKING BLOOD TO SURVIVE. I WILL DESTROY YOU!
GO AHEAD AND *TRY,* BROTHER.
AAAAAAA
KBOOM

YOU HAVE NO POWER OVER ME. GIVE UP.
YES, PERHAPS YOU ARE RIGHT. LET ME SAY A FINAL GOODBYE WITH A KISS.
GOODBYE MY BROTHER.
ETHAN, GRAB THE FLAME!
JUST AS WE ENTERED THIS WORLD, SO SHALL WE LEAVE... TOGETHER.
NO, LET GO OF ME. DO NOT...
BOOOOM

KRRRRRRRR

SEDNA, ***NO!***
I AM SORRY, CAT. I WILL ALWAYS LOVE YOU.
AND I YOU.
IT'S OVER.
WHAT HAPPENED?
I DON'T KNOW. AND WHY ARE WE AT THE TOWER OF LONDON?
LILY, I AM SO RRY FOR TURNING BACK ON YOU. I LOVE YOU!
YOU ARE A GOOD MAN, ETHAN CHANDLER. I BELIEVE I HAVE FINALLY SERVED MY PURPOSE. TIME FOR ME TO PASS OVER TO THE OTHER SIDE.
YOU WILL ALWAYS BE MY ONE AND ONLY FATHER, MALCOLM. GO IN PEACE.

HELLO, FATHER. WE HAVE BEEN WAITING PATIENTLY FOR YOU.
WHAT ON EARTH ARE YOU DOING HERE? I THOUGHT YOU FLED THE CITY.
FINDING A HOME WHEN YOU LOOK LIKE A MONSTER PROVED DIFFICULT FOR ME.
WHAT DO YOU WANT FROM ME?
I WANT NOTHING FROM YOU. IT'S MY FRIEND...HE NEEDS YOUR HELP.
KRRRSSS
HELLO, OLD C
I'M IN NEED OF
SERVICE.

REE WEEKS LATER
I AM BEREFT WITH EXCITEMENT TO SEE YOU, MY DEAR CAT.
MR. LYLE, OU ARE BUT A Y OF SUNSHINE. AM SO HAPPY YOU HAVE RECOVERED.
AND YOU AS WELL. I BELIEVE YOU ARE THE CAT WITH NINE LIVES. HOPE YOU STILL HAVE A FEW MORE LEFT.
LET'S HOPE. AND HOW IS YOUR WOUND? HEALING, I PRAY.
LUCKILY I AM MEATY, SO NOT TOO MUCH DAMAGE. THE ONLY NIBBLES I WANT ON MY NECK SHOULD BE FROM A SUITOR.
IT APPEARS THE MUSEUM SUSTAINED ONLY MINOR DAMAGE FROM THE FIRES.
TRAGIC WHAT HAPPENED TO THE REST OF THE CITY. BUT THROUGH THE ASHES WE RISE. OH -- AND SPEAKING OF RISEN, HAVE YOU HEARD THE AMAZING NEWS?
WHAT NEWS?
AN EXPLORER NAMED ARTERMAIN, QUITE A HANDSOME EVIL, RECENTLY DISCOVERED THIS *ST* FASCINATING COFFIN. DATE OF ORIGIN UNKNOWN, BUT MIGHT BE ORE THE BRONZE AGE. IT IS MADE OF A PURE STONE. CAN YOU BELIEVE IT?
WHERE WAS THIS COFFIN DISCOVERED?
OFF THE COAST F SCOTLAND, NEAR THE GHLANDS. IT WAS SUNKEN THE BOTTOM OF SOME SINISTER LAKE. THOSE ERRIFYING EARTHQUAKES MUST HAVE SET IT LOOSE.
MOR
THE INSCRIPTION IS LATIN. *MORS EST ILLIS APERIRE.*
"DEATH TO THOSE THAT OPEN." LYLE, THIS IS ***LILITH'S*** TOMB. PROMISE ME, WHATEVER YOU DO, PLEASE ***NEVER*** OPEN IT!

WE MADE IT, ETHAN. FINALLY, WE CAN START OUR NEW LIFE. YOU, ME, AND OUR PRECIOUS LITTLE GIRLS.
I PROMISE THAT NOTHING BAD SHALL EVER HAPPEN TO US AGAIN... I WILL ALWAYS PROTECT MY FAMILY.
I LOVE YOU, ETHAN. ...AND WOULD YOU LOOK AT THIS GLORIOUS CITY? STUNNING.
IT FEELS GOOD TO BE HOME.
THE END...FOR

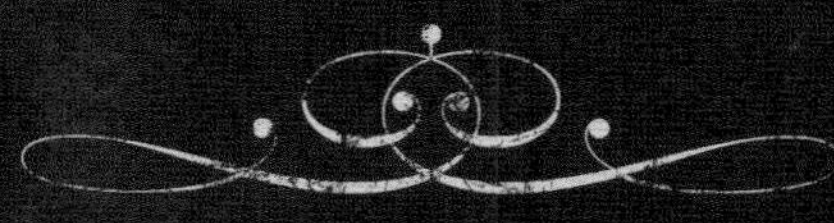

PENNY DREADFUL

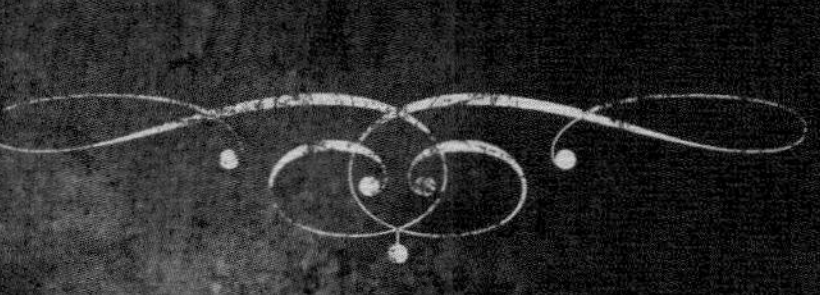

INKS

THE STUNNING BLACK AND WHITE
(AND RED) INTERIOR ARTWORK OF
JESÚS HERVÁS

SPLUT

COVERS GALLERY

#2.9 COVER A
TESS FOWLER

#2.9 COVER B
PHOTO

#2.9 COVER C
CLAUDIA IANNICIELLO

#2.10 COVER A
LENKA ŠIMEČKOVÁ

#2.10 COVER B
PHOTO

#2.11 COVER A
ROBERTA INGRANATA

#2.11 COVER B
PHOTO

#2.12 COVER A
ROBERTA INGRANATA

CREATOR BIOGRAPHIES

JOHN LOGAN is the creator, writer, and co-executive producer of *Penny Dreadful.* An American playwright, screenwriter, film and television producer, and a Golden Globe winner and two-time Academy Award-nominee, *Alien: Covenant, Spectre, Skyfall, Hugo, Any Given Sunday,* and *Gladiator* are among his best-known screenplays.

CHRIS KING is the co-executive producer of *Penny Dreadful,* with many more Hollywood credits to his name. He is perhaps best known for his work on the acclaimed documentaries *Foo Fighters: Back and Forth* and *Comics Superheroes Unmasked.*

JESÚS HERVÁS is a Spanish comic book artist known for *Sons of Anarchy, Androides,* and *Hitman: Agent 47.*

JASON WORDIE is a Canadian comics artist and colorist, who has lent his talents to *Paknadel and Trakhanvo's Turncoat* for BOOM! Studios and *God Country* for Image.

ROB STEEN is a veteran letterer of titles like *The Troop, Dark Souls, Astro City* and *X-Men.*

COMPLETE YOUR PENNY DREADFUL COLLECTION!

CONTINUING THE HIT TV SHOW
PENNY DREADFUL
BASED ON THE SERIES CREATED BY JOHN LOGAN

BARRIE PUBLIC LIBRARY
3 1862 50377 766 2

As the relics of an evil long since ... vanquished emerge from the darkness, the legacy of Vanessa Ives' death is clear: A battle is coming, and the victor shall show no mercy!

CONTINUING THE HIT TV SHOW
PENNY DREADFUL
BASED ON THE SERIES CREATED BY JOHN LOGAN
THE AWAKING • ARTIST'S EDITION
CHRIS KING • JESÚS HERVÁS • ROB STEEN

PENNY DREADFUL ARTIST'S EDITION VOL. 1: THE AWAKING

ISBN: 9781785868771

This black and white (and red) art edition of Penny Dreadful: The Awakening showcases the mesmerising original artwork of Jesús Hervás!

AVAILABLE IN PRINT AND DIGITALLY.

FIND OUT MORE AT TITAN-COMICS.COM

BARRIE PUBLIC LIBRARY
3 1862 50377 766 2

CONTINUING THE HIT TV SERIES!

The long, hidden war for the fate of mankind reaches new heights of terror, as the Mother of Evil, reincarnated in the body of Vanessa Ives, gathers dark powers and evil minds to strike one final time at the heart of humanity – the Antichrist is due. Discover the fates of Ethan, Lily, Cat, and many more – the end times have come at last!

"A SUCCESSOR ON PA WITH SHOWTIME'S CUL PHENOMENON!"

DIABOLIQUE MAGAZINE

"POSSIBLY THE BEST BOOK ON THE RACKS RIGHT NOW. UNMISSABLE!"

NERDLY

The first epic comics sequel to the critically-acclaimed SHOWTIME TV series concludes, written by the show's co-producer, Chris King, and astoundingly illustrated by Jesús Hervás (*Sons of Anarchy*) and Jason Wordie!

Collects #9-12 of the ongoing series.

ALSO AVAILABLE IN THIS SERIES

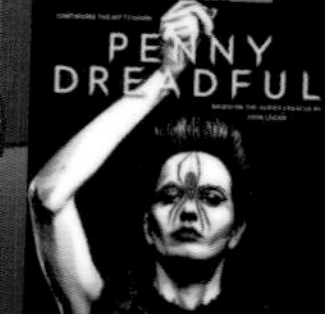

TITAN COMICS

GRAPHIC NOVEL
$16.99 US
$22.99 CAN
£13.99 UK

SUGGESTED FOR MATURE READERS

ISBN: 9781785861437
51699
9 781785 861437

TITAN-COMICS.COM

RONT COVER ART PHOTO
ACK COVER ART BY TESS FOWLER

DC

Harley Quinn Black + White + Red